MW01174219

Symphony of *Survival* in the Key of "C"

Keeping Marital **Commitment** Strong

CHARLES R. SWINDOLL

INSIGHT FOR LIVING

SYMPHONY OF SURVIVAL IN THE KEY OF "C"
Keeping Marital Commitment Strong
By Charles R. Swindoll

Charles R. Swindoll has devoted his life to the clear, practical teaching and application of God's Word and His grace. A pastor at heart, Chuck has served as senior pastor to congregations in Texas, Massachusetts, and California. He currently pastors Stonebriar Community Church in Frisco, Texas, but Chuck's listening audience extends far beyond a local church body. As a leading program in Christian broadcasting, *Insight for Living* airs in major Christian radio markets around the world, reaching people groups in languages they can understand. Chuck's extensive writing ministry has also served the body of Christ worldwide and his leadership as president and now chancellor of Dallas Theological Seminary has helped prepare and equip a new generation for ministry. Chuck and Cynthia, his partner in life and ministry, have four grown children and ten grandchildren.

Copyright © 2006, 2011 by Charles R. Swindoll, Inc.

The text of this booklet was taken from chapter 3 of *Marriage: From Surviving to Thriving: Practical Advice on Making Your Marriage Stronger*, copyright © 2006 by Charles R. Swindoll, Inc. (Nashville: Thomas Nelson, 2006) 57–77.

Published By:
IFL Publishing House, A Division of Insight for Living,
Post Office Box 251007, Plano, Texas 75025-1007

Editor in Chief: Cynthia Swindoll, President, Insight for Living
Executive Vice President: Wayne Stiles, Th.M., D.Min., Dallas Theological Seminary
Editor: John Adair, Th.M., Ph.D., Dallas Theological Seminary
Copy Editors: Jim Craft, M.A., English, Mississippi College
Kathryn Merritt, M.A., English, Hardin-Simmons University
Project Coordinator, Creative Ministries: Melanie Munnell, M.A., Humanities, The University of Texas at Dallas
Project Coordinator, Communications: Sarah Magnoni, A.A.S., University of Wisconsin
Proofreader: Paula McCoy, B.A., English, Texas A&M University-Commerce
Intern: Kirby Grigsby, student, Rhodes College
Cover Designer: Laura Dubroc, B.F.A., Advertising Design, University of Louisiana at Lafayette
Production Artist: Nancy Gustine, B.F.A., Advertising Art, University of North Texas
Back Cover Photo: David Edmonson

ISBN: 978-1-57972-926-4
Printed in the United States of America

Symphony of *Survival* in the Key of "C"

Keeping Marital **Commitment** Strong

A Letter from Chuck

I love the Olympics. Every four years, world-class athletes gather in one place to compete with the best athletes on earth. Some come in heavily favored and fulfill every expectation. I think of swimmer Michael Phelps and his eight gold medals at the 2008 Olympics. Others come in as underdogs, yet their results often exceed every expectation. I immediately think of the United States hockey team, who defeated the mighty Soviets for the gold medal at the 1980 Olympics.

Whether it's that of a favorite or an underdog, the path to success follows the same game plan: never back down, never quit, hang tough, keep hammering away, stay at it, regardless.

In a word: *commitment.*

In our permissive, irresponsible, and escapist world, *commitment* is almost a dirty word. Those who would rather rationalize and run than stick with it and watch God pull off a miracle or two (not to mention reshape us in the process) resist this whole concept.

Marriage isn't begun in a context of vagueness and uncertainty. Two people, fully conscious, very much awake and aware, declare their vows. I realize that vows vary, but without exception, they include phrases such as "for better or for worse" or "'til death do us part."

Right? Remember those words you promised before God? Did He hear you? I'm being facetious—*of course He heard you!* Read for yourself: "When you make a vow to God, do not be late in paying it; for He takes no delight in fools. Pay what you vow!" (Ecclesiastes 5:4).

Yes, He not only takes those words seriously, He remembers them permanently. A vow is a vow. No amount of psychological therapy, positive thinking (often dubbed "grace"), semantic footwork with the biblical text, alternative concepts, or mutual support from family and friends can remove your responsibility to keep your word. Yes, there are a few exceptions . . . but by and large, you are responsible to keep your marriage vows.

But, you say, *it's difficult*. Of course it's difficult! There will be times when you are convinced you can't go on. But I remind you of your vow, your stated commitment before God: "*for better, for worse.*" I hope this booklet on the topic of commitment helps you see clearly your responsibility, your marriage, and most of all, the God you love and seek to serve well.

Commitment is not just another word. It is *the* watchword for a struggling, hurting, eroding marriage that seems destined to be locked up and closed forever.

Commitment is the key.

Charles R. Swindoll

Symphony of *Survival* in the Key of "C"

Keeping Marital **Commitment** Strong

I am more than 75 years old, I have been married for more than fifty-five years, and I have been in ministry for more than forty-five years. So when I speak to a twenty-first-century audience, I sometimes find it challenging to sound like something other than a nineteenth-century preacher! I discovered that there's a word for guys like me, a preacher who still believes the Bible, who thinks we need to adjust our lives to the principles of Scripture rather than twist the text to justify our choices. Someone told me that when I'm not around, a few people call me a "dinosaur." So, as often happens, my curiosity sent me to the dictionary:

> di•no•saur \'d -n -,sor\ noun . . . **3**: one that is impractically large, out-of-date, or obsolete[1]

I was admittedly a little dismayed, but I found it easier to stomach than the Greek etymology of the word: *deinos* + *sauros* . . . "terrifying lizard." After I mentioned this to a group of people, a man offered me a little comfort. "I wouldn't feel too bad if I were you. One of my grandkids calls me a Neanderthal!" I'm afraid to look that one up.

Aside from being "impractically large," I'm proud to be a dinosaur, especially if that means remaining faithful to God's Word—believing it, studying it, diligently preparing and passionately delivering messages that reflect its timeless principles. In a postmodern generation that gropes for truth, it's reassuring to cling to what I know to be reliable.

Unfortunately, some tend to mistake this confidence for arrogance. Such are our times. G. K. Chesterton saw the early signs of this many years ago when he wrote:

> But what we suffer from today is humility in the wrong place. Modesty has moved from the organ of ambition. Modesty has settled upon the organ of conviction; where it was never meant to be. A man was meant to be doubtful about himself, but undoubting about the truth; this has been exactly reversed. . . . We are on the road to reproducing a race of men too mentally modest to believe in the multiplication table.[2]

We need to be absolutely sure of what we believe, especially if our marriages are going to stand the test of time. I don't claim to be the author or the sole possessor of truth. But I can say with assurance that I embrace the truth without apology or hesitation. Many centuries old and available in almost any bookstore, the Bible is full of unusual names and stories too bizarre to be fiction, preserving ideas as profound as they are ancient. In the pages of the Bible, we find principles for living—unique in their presentation, plainly wrapped in elegant simplicity, yet deeply mysterious and profound.

These principles are reliable. We can trust them to preserve us and our relationships however unsophisticated they may appear to the intellectual mind. The text of the Bible was originally written in Hebrew and Aramaic and Greek, authored and assembled over hundreds of years by a variety of people—all of them human and therefore sinful—yet God has miraculously preserved the accuracy and relevance of its truth. Consequently, it has the authority to instruct any society, in any era, in any region.

God's Word will help people of any age, any social status, in any life stage or circumstance: married, single, widowed, divorced, abused, broken, terrorized, hurting, struggling, fighting for survival, prosperous, happy, healthy, joyful, guilty, grieving, or dying. In more than fifty years of study, I have never found an irrelevant principle in the pages of Scripture. Anytime I have found one that I thought had failed me, it was because I failed to understand, appreciate, and apply it. In the end, I discovered that I had failed the principle rather than the other way around. And the consequences were usually grave.

Every biblically based marriage requires principles that inform how couples order their lives. One of the most significant marriage principles leads to permanence between a couple. It's simple, straightforward, highly effective, and, like me, something of a dinosaur. The principle can be summed up in a single word: *commitment*.

Commitment: The Key to a Permanent Marriage

*T*here's nothing fancy about the word *commitment*—a simple word that describes a simple concept. Now as a realist, I recognize that simple doesn't mean easy. And I am not so naive and rigid in my theology as to ignore the fact that we live in a world twisted by evil as a result of Genesis 3, and certain circumstances call for separation and even allow for divorce.

But that's not where we begin. One author noted that divorce, like embalming, is not something you want to apply prematurely. I discuss the biblical grounds for divorce and remarriage in another booklet, *Divorce & Remarriage: A Biblical Perspective*; so we'll not dwell on it here. I want to focus on the reasons to *stay* rather than the reasons to *escape*.

Commitment is a biblical mandate for marriage. And like all biblical mandates, it requires faith to see beyond the immediate and offers unseen rewards when obeyed. Take it from a guy who's been married for more than fifty-five years: that one-flesh union won't maintain itself, but it's worth the effort. You *learn* to become a unit. You stay with it through all of the sinful struggles and annoying habits, plodding through those hard times when you would like nothing more than to call it quits and disappear. Then, after you've made it through a number of crises together, you realize in unguarded moments that you're glad you stuck it out. You're glad you made it work. And you're especially glad your husband or wife didn't walk out.

As we examine commitment, the key to permanence, three couples in the Bible come to mind. Each faced a particular challenge and has something to teach us by their example.

The Challenge of Consequences
(Adam and Eve)

$\mathcal{T}$he marriage of Adam and Eve in Genesis 2, like most weddings, took place under ideal circumstances. But unlike any other marriage, they were married by God in a pristine environment, in a world without sin. "The man and his wife were both naked and were not ashamed" (Genesis 2:25). Nothing inhibited their intimacy. No hint of selfishness tainted their caring for each other. No outburst of anger led them into a verbal fight.

Then sin changed all of that. After their disobedience, God detailed the consequences of their tragic choice:

> To the woman he said, "I will greatly increase your labor pains; with pain you will give birth to children. You will want to control your husband, but he will dominate you." But to Adam he said, "Because you obeyed your wife and ate from the tree about which I commanded you, 'You must not eat from it,' cursed is the ground thanks to you; in painful toil you will eat of it all the days of your life. It will produce thorns and thistles

for you, but you will eat the grain of the field. By the sweat of your brow you will eat food until you return to the ground for out of it you were taken; for you are dust, and to dust you will return." . . . So the Lord God expelled him from the orchard in Eden to cultivate the ground from which he had been taken. (Genesis 3:16–19, 23 NET)

This is what theologians call "the fall." It affected the nature of humankind, their relationships, and even the world around them. Nothing is destroyed, but everything is damaged. Because of sin, there's something wrong with everything. But notice what did *not* change. The man and woman still bore the image of God, though that image became a contorted one. They were still to care for the earth, but it would resist their efforts. Humanity's relationship with the ground would be hampered by difficulty—thistles and weeds—and the soil would only yield produce through sweat and toil. The same would be true of their relationship. They remained husband and wife and were still to multiply and fill the earth. Yet what had been an easy, natural intimacy became complicated by fear and defensiveness, selfishness and withdrawal. And the awful effects of sin would continue to haunt them.

They were driven from the garden of Eden, never again to see the idyllic place of their pairing and first wonderful days of their marriage. They would bury a son, the victim of murder at the hands of his older brother. They would see their eldest son banished from all social contact, cursed to live as a vagrant because of his crime. And, if my calculations are correct, Adam lived long enough to attend the birth of Noah, which means that the first couple saw the steady moral decline of the world's inhabitants (their own descendants) to the point that God regretted creating people at all.

If anyone could cite difficulties as a reason to end their marriage, Adam and Eve could. Yet through it all, they remained together. We learn from the marriage of Adam and Eve that the harsh consequences of evil—the sin-corrupted image of God in humans and the sin-twisted world—do not make marriage impossible. Difficult but not impossible.

You may have come from a home so unbelievably horrific that few can comprehend the damage it has done to you. You may bear deep scars of abuse and mistreatment—emotional, physical, perhaps even sexual. You may have come from a household where you never knew the safety and security of parents who loved each other and loved you. Maybe you haven't seen a healthy marriage modeled for you, which means you don't even know how to begin building one. Maybe your romantic life is one characterized by a long string of broken relationships with poorly chosen partners and sabotage at the first sign of genuine intimacy.

If you are married and this describes you — even just a little — take heart. Healing is available. It won't be easy, but you'll never find it by running. If you are married and if your safety isn't threatened, choose to remain committed to your mate as an important first step.

The Challenge of Conflict (Hosea and Gomer)

I can think of no greater challenge to marriage than infidelity. So serious is the damage that the Lord considers it a breach of the marital bond and permits divorce (Matthew 19:8–9). However, that's not to say that divorce is required or even inevitable. Consider the marriage of the prophet Hosea.

Many centuries after Adam and Eve and long after Moses, the judges, and King David, Israel was living in Canaan. But sin and idolatry plunged the nation into civil war, dividing north from south, with the northern kingdom worshiping other gods. To convict the Hebrew people of their spiritual infidelity, God chose to use the life of His prophet Hosea—not only his words and his writing but his *marriage*.

> When the LORD first spoke through Hosea, the Lord said to Hosea, "Go, take to yourself a wife of harlotry and have children of harlotry; for the land commits flagrant harlotry, forsaking the LORD." (Hosea 1:2)

What an amazing command! This was a costly object lesson for Hosea and introduces one of the most difficult books of Scripture to read and to interpret. To get His point across, the Lord put Himself in the role of a jilted spouse and walked with His servant Hosea through the horrifying experience of marital infidelity. The Lord knows the sting of betrayal firsthand and on a scale we can barely comprehend.

> So he went and took Gomer the daughter of Diblaim, and she conceived and bore him a son. (1:3)

Scholars cannot say for sure whether Gomer was a harlot before marriage or became one some years later. The phrase "wife of harlotry" seems to describe what she would become because she was not a wife at the time Hosea chose her, and the "children of harlotry" had not yet been born. So we might say he picked a nice, Hebrew girl to marry.

> Then she conceived again and gave birth to a daughter. And the Lord said to him, "Name her Lo-ruhamah, for I will no longer have compassion on the house of Israel, that I would ever forgive them." (Hosea 1:6)

The name of the daughter means literally "no compassion." The names of the children are symbolic, which was very common for the time. The name of each child describes God's attitude toward Israel. The boy's name, Jezreel, points to the nation's violent behavior. The girl's name warns that the Lord's patience with wayward Israel was running out. Then Gomer bore another boy.

> When she had weaned Lo-ruhamah, she conceived and gave birth to a son. And the Lord said, "Name him Lo-ammi, for you are not My people and I am not your God." (1:8–9)

Lo-ammi means "not my people." At this point, Gomer apparently left Hosea to live a life of prostitution. In a very real sense, she was no longer his wife. Hosea 2 describes Israel in these same terms, which reflected Gomer's behavior. She gave herself to multiple men, living off the money she bartered for sex. Meanwhile, Hosea was left a single parent with the responsibilities of rearing the children alone. He was a prophet of God who had to carry on with ministry despite his embarrassment before others and the deep hurt he felt. I have a preacher friend who calls this story "A Scandal in the Parsonage." Indeed it was.

At this point, it's safe to say that the marriage was over. Put bluntly, Gomer became a whore on the street, which gave Hosea every moral cause to divorce her. The Bible doesn't tell us whether or not he did this. Nevertheless, her actions made it clear that she was no longer living with him as his wife.

Then something remarkable happens in chapter 3. We have no way of knowing how long Gomer was gone. She may have lived as a prostitute for many years. Aging, used up, and pathetic, she could have sold herself into slavery to survive — a common practice for the destitute. It was then that the Lord instructed Hosea to do the unthinkable.

The LORD said to me, "Go, show love to your wife again, even though she loves another man and continually commits adultery. Likewise, the LORD loves the Israelites although they turn to other gods and love to offer raisin cakes to idols." So I paid fifteen shekels of silver and about seven bushels of barley to purchase her. (Hosea 3:1–2 NET)

This was the normal price for a slave.

Then I told her, "You must live with me many days; you must not commit adultery or have sexual intercourse with another man, and I also will wait for you." (3:3 NET)

I find his words to her utterly remarkable.

I don't want to lose sight of the bigger issue here. This is, first, a picture of the Lord's relationship with Israel. Hosea 9:9 says, "[The nation has] gone deep in depravity." On a national scale, they left the Lord to prostitute themselves with false gods. And, like Hosea, the Lord in grace purchased them back at great cost to Himself and restored them to their former place of honor as His people. (This is clearly a foreshadowing of what Christ would do on the cross for you and me.)

What Hosea did for his unfaithful and undeserving wife is a prime example of uncommon grace. He was directed to do this by God because he had a very unique duty as the Lord's spokesman before Israel. So his case is special. However, it does represent God's highest, greatest desire in such cases. This is important for all of us to keep in mind—for those who have suffered the betrayal of marital infidelity *and* for those who haven't.

I write these next few lines very sensitively. Please read them slowly and carefully. If you are the victim of marital infidelity—probably the greatest challenge to a marriage—you are not *required* by Scripture to remain married. God does permit divorce in this case. However, if your mate is genuinely repentant and willing to do the difficult work of rebuilding the trust, let me encourage you to consider applying uncommon grace. Hosea did . . . and so can you. While you are entitled to walk away, you may be forfeiting greater happiness and healing that come by extending grace than by turning away and claiming your right. It's a more difficult path, admittedly. It's riskier. It requires immense faith and enormous forgiveness. But unseen rewards could be greater than you can imagine. Divorce will not erase the pain and the damage the infidelity has done to your spirit. You must heal either way. The question is how and with whom will you heal?

For those who haven't suffered this horrible tragedy, Hosea's example demonstrates that no marriage is "too dead" for the Lord to restore. All marriages have at least one thing in common: *they all involve sinful people*. Sooner or later, one spouse will sin against the other and sin big. Sin, forgiveness, healing, and rebuilding trust challenge the commitment of every marriage. If the Lord put the marriage of Hosea and Gomer back together, He can keep yours from falling apart in the face of just about anything.

The Challenges of Circumstances (Joseph and Mary)

A third example can be found tucked away in the first chapter of Matthew's gospel. It's a familiar story told every Christmas, but I want to look at this story through a different lens.

> Now the birth of Jesus Christ was as follows: when His mother Mary had been betrothed to Joseph, before they came together she was found

to be with child by the Holy Spirit.
(Matthew 1:18)

According to the Jewish custom of the time, Mary and Joseph were formally united by a marriage contract but were required to wait one year before consummating the marriage, celebrating the official public wedding, and setting up their own household. The contract was so binding, however, that only a legal divorce could break it. Mary was considered Joseph's wife in every respect. During this period, before Joseph had ever touched her intimately, Mary became pregnant.

We know from Luke's account that Mary was made aware of the plan; an angel explained to her what was going to happen. The Holy Spirit miraculously conceived her child. However, Joseph knew nothing ahead of time. All he knew was that Mary was pregnant with a child that was not his. Take note of his response:

> And Joseph her husband, being a righteous man and not wanting to disgrace her, planned to send her away secretly. But when he had considered this, behold, an angel of the Lord appeared to him in a dream, saying, "Joseph, son of

David, do not be afraid to take Mary as your wife; for the Child who has been conceived in her is of the Holy Spirit. She will bear a Son; and you shall call His name Jesus, for He will save His people from their sins."
(Matthew 1:19–21)

Try hard to identify with what Joseph must have felt. He discovered that his wife was pregnant, drew the only conclusion that made sense—adultery, and decided to opt for a quiet divorce. Mary probably tried to explain, but let's face it: her story is unbelievable. "Yes, I'm pregnant; no, I didn't have sex with another man. God caused all of this, Joseph."

Come on! *No man* would believe that.

Thankfully, Joseph soon received confirmation from God that Mary had told him the truth. Then came the decision. He had to know that any hope for a normal marriage would be frustrated by the inevitable wagging of tongues. The neighborhood gossip network in the small town of Nazareth would be working overtime. Everyone in his community could count to nine, and when Mary showed up at the synagogue in maternity clothes a little sooner than expected, everyone would reach the same conclusion. Talk about a scandal! We know this happened because, later in Jesus's ministry, His enemies in the temple said with biting sarcasm, "*We* were not born of fornication" (John 8:41, emphasis added).

Joseph and Mary would have to rest confidently in the truth of their innocence and find contentment in that. No one would believe the truth, no matter how hard they tried to convince them. Whispers, snickers, jokes, and scorn would be their closest and most enduring companions. This would either draw them together, or it would become a wedge. They would either seek opposite corners of the house or turn toward each other for strength. Stop and think. Everything hinged on their commitment to each other.

If the couple remained committed, their marriage would endure the strangest circumstances. No one outside the couple would understand (including their parents), and the married pair might be left with no external support. But if they remained committed to each other and the covenant they made with God, the marriage would survive. In fact, the intimacy may have grown sweeter as the two shared a perspective that no one else on earth would appreciate.

You may be faced with an unusual set of circumstances that challenges your marriage from the outside. Having been in ministry for more than four decades, I've helped a lot of folks going through terrible times. So I know how difficult life can be when dealing with problems in a marriage. Nevertheless, in all these years, I've never seen one marriage get worse when the partners redoubled their commitment to each other. The problems may not have gone away, but the marriage only got stronger.

An Important Disclaimer

I feel the need to insert a qualification to everything I have written so far. I want to remain biblical to the core but without being so rigid as to ignore some ugly realities. In fact, the Bible doesn't ignore them either. My heart has been broken more than a few times when I witnessed situations in which a divorce averted certain disaster.

If you or your children are in danger of physical harm, you have a moral obligation to put an end to the relationship as it exists now. Reconciliation or remarriage are issues that can be dealt with in due time. For the sake of yourself and your children, get out, get away, and get help. Divorce may or may not be the right course of action, depending upon your mate's willingness or ability to change. But unless and until the marriage is safe, depart *and remain* apart. The Lord never intended your commitment to be your destruction. God is firm, but He isn't cruel.

If your married partner is using illegal drugs, I highly recommend that you at least separate until he or she has demonstrated the ability to remain clean and sober for a number of months. Remain committed. This is part of the vows, but you would be foolish to live in the same household.

If your mate is committing adultery, continues the sinful behavior, and remains unrepentant, your commitment to the marriage may actually discourage reconciliation. This sounds strange, but I encourage you to read a fine book by my good friend Dr. James Dobson titled *Love Must Be Tough*. He goes into careful detail that I'll not attempt to go into in this booklet. I must warn you . . . it won't be easy. Doing what's right in difficult situations is never easy.

Keeping the Marriage under Lock and Key

If a marriage is going to survive, commitment is priority one. Very little else you do in a marriage will matter if you haven't determined to stay in it. Whether the challenge is consequences, conflict, or circumstances, the key to maintaining a lifelong marriage is commitment. It's a choice that doesn't change with feelings, doesn't depend on good fortune, and doesn't rely on the attitude of your mate. Commitment says to your partner, "I know things have gone sour, I know you have sinned and I have sinned, I know that these are rough times, but I will remain with you regardless."

Your soft-beating heart under a moonlit sky in Hawaii won't keep you together. The lovely ceremony and the heartfelt vows you spoke are memories you hold dear, but they tend to fade in the harsh light of the world's challenges. It's a decision you make, once for all time, and then confirm with your actions each day. It's a simple concept that's anything but easy . . . but no more complicated than making the decision to stay.

The following is a letter from a woman who heard me speak on commitment several years ago. Her words illustrate the simple power of this difficult decision.

> I've decided to remain steadfast in commitment to my own marriage that was in the middle of a divorce

action. . . . God has changed me. He has given me a new love for my husband and, in turn, my husband has been changing in his attitude toward me. He's still uncommitted about his relationship with Jesus—a miracle I am anticipating.

Six months ago, we sat and listened to a non-Christian counselor tell us to get on with the divorce because there was absolutely nothing left in our marriage and no basis upon which to build.

Well, God's grace has allowed the contrary. It's still a real struggle some days, but I've learned that as we "pull" toward each other rather than "push" at each other, the direction is more secure and sound.

So, *commitment* is not just another word in my vocabulary. It's become a real part of my life.

One final "C"-word in this symphony of survival: *Christ.* If commitment is the key, then Christ is the lock. I'm amazed that any marriage between nonbelievers lasts very long. Some do last, but I'm always surprised that marriages without Christ don't end sooner. However, if both partners remain steadfastly committed to Christ, regardless, a lasting marriage can become a reality. With His presence in our lives, His transforming power, His constant encouragement, and His infectious compassion steadily working to make us more like Him, how can a marriage fail?

How to Begin a Relationship with God

*R*emaining committed to your spouse can, at times, seem like a daunting task. The hardships of marriage can leave you both feeling hopeless and struggling to remain faithful to your vows.

In order to survive and thrive, your marriage needs a solid foundation established in Jesus Christ. If you and your spouse do not maintain the same Christian beliefs, your marriage is like a house built upon sand instead of solid ground—unstable and easily torn apart. As Christians, we rely upon and trust in God to fulfill and support our marriage bonds through each spouse's strong relationship with Him. When the going gets tough, we can count on God to provide strength and peace.

God does not promise to save your marriage just because you become a Christian, but He will save *you*! And that can't help but affect all your other relationships. How can you begin this wonderful relationship with Jesus? The Bible marks the path with four essential truths. Let's look at each marker in detail.

Our Spiritual Condition:
Totally Depraved

The first truth is rather personal. One look in the mirror of Scripture, and our human condition becomes painfully clear:

> "There is none righteous, not even one;
> There is none who understands,
> There is none who seeks for God;
> All have turned aside, together they
>   have become useless;
> There is none who does good,
> There is not even one."
>   (Romans 3:10–12)

We are all sinners through and through—totally depraved. Now, that doesn't mean we've committed every atrocity known to humankind. We're not as *bad* as we can be, just as *bad off* as we can be. Sin colors all our thoughts, motives, words, and actions.

If you've been around a while, you likely already believe it. Look around. Everything around us bears the smudge marks of our sinful nature. Despite our best efforts to create a perfect world, crime statistics continue to soar, divorce rates keep climbing, and families keep crumbling.

Something has gone terribly wrong in our society and in ourselves—something deadly. Contrary to how the world would repackage it, "me-first" living doesn't equal rugged individuality and freedom; it equals death. As Paul said in his letter to the Romans, "The wages of sin is death" (Romans 6:23)—our spiritual and physical death that comes from God's righteous judgment of our sin, along with all of the emotional and practical effects of this separation that we experience on a daily basis. This brings us to the second marker: God's character.

God's Character: Infinitely Holy

How can God judge us for a sinful state we were born into? Our total depravity is only half the answer. The other half is God's infinite holiness.

The fact that we know things are not as they should be points us to a standard of goodness beyond ourselves. Our sense of injustice in life on this side of eternity implies a perfect standard of justice beyond our reality. That standard and source is God Himself. And God's standard of holiness contrasts starkly with our sinful condition.

Scripture says that "God is Light, and in Him there is no darkness at all" (1 John 1:5). God is absolutely holy — which creates a problem for us. If He is so pure, how can we who are so impure relate to Him?

Perhaps we could try being better people, try to tilt the balance in favor of our good deeds, or seek out methods for self-improvement. Throughout history, people have attempted to live up to God's standard by keeping the Ten Commandments or living by their own code of ethics. Unfortunately, no one can come close to satisfying the demands of God's law. Romans 3:20 says, "By the works of the Law no flesh will be justified in His sight; for through the Law comes the knowledge of sin."

Our Need: A Substitute

So here we are, sinners by nature and sinners by choice, trying to pull ourselves up by our own bootstraps to attain a relationship with our holy Creator. But every time we try, we fall flat on our faces. We can't live a good enough life to make up for our sin, because God's standard isn't "good enough" — it's *perfection*. And we can't make amends for the offense our sin has created without dying for it.

Who can get us out of this mess?

If someone could live perfectly, honoring God's law, and would bear sin's death penalty for us—in our place—then we would be saved from our predicament. But is there such a person? Thankfully, yes!

Meet your substitute—*Jesus Christ*. He is the One who took death's place for you!

> [God] made [Jesus Christ] who knew no sin to be sin on our behalf, so that we might become the righteousness of God in Him. (2 Corinthians 5:21)

God's Provision: A Savior

God rescued us by sending His Son, Jesus, to die on the cross for our sins (1 John 4:9–10). Jesus was fully human and fully divine (John 1:1, 18), a truth that ensures His understanding of our weaknesses, His power to forgive, and His ability to bridge the gap between God and us (Romans 5:6–11). In short, we are "justified as a gift by His grace through the redemption which is in Christ Jesus" (Romans 3:24). Two words in this verse bear further explanation: *justified* and *redemption*.

Justification is God's act of mercy, in which He declares righteous the believing sinners while we are still in our sinning state. Justification doesn't mean that God *makes* us righteous, so that we never sin again, rather that He *declares* us righteous—much like a judge pardons a guilty criminal. Because Jesus took our sin upon Himself and suffered our judgment on the cross, God forgives our debt and proclaims us PARDONED.

Redemption is Christ's act of paying the complete price to release us from sin's bondage. God sent His Son to bear His wrath for all of our sins—past, present, and future (Romans 3:24–26; 2 Corinthians 5:21). In humble obedience, Christ willingly endured the shame of the cross for our sake (Mark 10:45; Romans 5:6–8; Philippians 2:8). Christ's death satisfied God's righteous demands. He no longer holds our sins against us, because His own Son paid the penalty for them. We are freed from the slave market of sin, never to be enslaved again!

Placing Your Faith in Christ

These four truths describe how God has provided a way to Himself through Jesus Christ. Because the price has been paid in full by God, we must respond to His free gift of eternal life in total faith and confidence in Him to save us. We must step forward into the relationship with God that He has prepared for us — not by doing good works or by being a good person, but by coming to Him just as we are and accepting His justification and redemption by faith.

> For by grace you have been saved through faith; and that not of your-selves, it is the gift of God; not as a result of works, so that no one may boast. (Ephesians 2:8 – 9)

We accept God's gift of salvation simply by placing our faith in Christ alone for the forgiveness of our sins. Would you like to enter a relationship with your Creator by trusting in Christ as your Savior? If so, here's a simple prayer you can use to express your faith:

> *Dear God,*
>
> *I know that my sin has put a barrier between You and me. Thank You for sending Your Son, Jesus, to die in my place. I trust in Jesus alone to forgive my sins, and I accept His gift of eternal life. I ask Jesus to be my personal Savior and the Lord of my life. Thank You. In Jesus's name, amen.*

If you've prayed this prayer or one like it and you wish to find out more about knowing God and His plan for you in the Bible, contact us at Insight for Living. Our contact information is on the following pages.

We Are Here for You

If you desire to find out more about knowing God and His plan for you in the Bible, contact us. Insight for Living provides staff pastors who are available for free written correspondence or phone consultation. These seminary-trained and seasoned counselors have years of experience and are well-qualified guides for your spiritual journey.

Please feel welcome to contact your regional Pastoral Ministries by using the information below:

United States
Insight for Living
Pastoral Ministries
Post Office Box 269000
Plano, Texas 75026-9000
USA
972-473-5097, Monday through Friday,
8:00 a.m. – 5:00 p.m. central time
www.insight.org/contactapastor

Canada

Insight for Living Canada

Pastoral Ministries

PO Box 8 Stn A

Abbotsford BC V2T 6Z4

CANADA

1-800-663-7639

info@insightforliving.ca

Australia, New Zealand, and South Pacific

Insight for Living Australia

Pastoral Care

Post Office Box 443

Boronia, VIC 3155

AUSTRALIA

1300 467 444

United Kingdom and Europe

Insight for Living United Kingdom

Pastoral Care

PO Box 553

Dorking

RH4 9EU

UNITED KINGDOM

0800 915 9364

+44 (0)1306 640156

pastoralcare@insightforliving.org.uk

Endnotes

1. *Merriam-Webster's Collegiate Dictionary*, 11th ed. (Springfield, Mass.: Merriam-Webster, 2007), see "dinosaur."

2. G. K. Chesterton, *Orthodoxy* (Wheaton, Ill.: Harold Shaw, 1994), 29, 30.

Ordering Information

If you would like to order additional copies of the *Symphony of Survival in the Key of "C"* booklet or order other Insight for Living resources, please contact the office that serves you.

United States
Insight for Living
Post Office Box 269000
Plano, Texas 75026-9000
USA
1-800-772-8888 (Monday through Friday, 7:00 a.m. – 7:00 p.m. central time)
www.insight.org
www.insightworld.org

Canada
Insight for Living Canada
PO Box 8 Stn A
Abbotsford BC V2T 6Z4
CANADA
1-800-663-7639
www.insightforliving.ca

Australia, New Zealand, and South Pacific

Insight for Living Australia

Post Office Box 443

Boronia, VIC 3155

AUSTRALIA

1300 467 444

www.insight.asn.au

United Kingdom and Europe

Insight for Living United Kingdom

PO Box 553

Dorking

RH4 9EU

UNITED KINGDOM

0800 915 9364

www.insightforliving.org.uk

Other International Locations

International constituents may contact
the U.S. office through our Web site
(www.insightworld.org), mail queries,
or by calling +1-972-473-5136.